TEACHERS' FAVORITES™

Fun Activities for SUMMER!

Reproducible Patterns for Paper Crafts, Coloring Pages, Games, Decorations, and More!

D1270765

Illustrations by Rick Ewigleben

Publications International, Ltd.

Introduction written by Holli Fort.

PIL grants the purchaser of this book the right to photocopy the pages of this book for one classroom set only. It is strictly prohibited to reproduce these pages for distribution to more than one classroom, an entire school, or a school district or for distribution for commercial resale. Permission is never granted for commercial purposes.

Teachers' Favorites is a trademark of Publications International, Ltd.

Louis Weber, CEO
Publications International, Ltd.
7373 North Cicero Avenue
Lincolnwood, Illinois 60712

Permission is never granted for commercial purposes.

ISBN-13: 978-1-60553-981-2
ISBN-10: 1-60553-981-3

Manufactured in U.S.A.

8 7 6 5 4 3 2 1

Contents

Beat the Heat with Cool Summer Fun!

It's easy enough to color a smiling sun or cut out a surfboard. But having inventive and engaging activities that students respond to, have fun with, and maybe even learn from can be a daunting task. This is true whether you lead a classroom, Sunday school class, scout troop, or a home filled with eager learners. The adaptable projects featured in *Teachers' Favorites*™: *Fun Activities for Summer!* will help you challenge your students with educational activities and purely fun seasonal projects.

Each season in this four-book series offers up a unique buffet of holidays, milestones, sports, and activities. Summer is the time for Father's Day, Independence Day, camping, volleyball, and stargazing. Students will enjoy relevant crafts that can be hung, worn, read, laminated, given as gifts, or used to decorate the room or bulletin board.

Teachers' Favorites™: *Fun Activities for Summer!* includes the following types of activities:

• Coloring
• Writing
• Math
• Paper crafts
• Games, such as look-and-find, connect the dots, and mazes

For craft projects, take the time to go over the instructions carefully. Also, make sure you have all the materials on hand before you get started. Here are just a few of the materials that are required for most projects:

Paper: Since the projects in this book will need to be photocopied for each student, be sure to have plenty of paper. Most projects can be copied on regular copy paper, but some projects (such as paper dolls and cutouts that stand) should be copied on heavier stock or construction paper. If you do not have access to heavier stock or your copier cannot accommodate construction paper, you can glue the project's paper to construction paper to make it sturdier. For some projects, such as the card for Father's Day, it is important that you can't see through the paper. In such cases, you might want to glue construction paper to the back of the paper.

Glue and tape: Some projects call for glue and/or clear tape. If you use glue, make sure it is water-base and nontoxic.

Scissors: Many projects call for cutting out pieces. Some require cutting slits or poking holes. For younger children, you may need to do the cutting yourself—or have older children help. Always have safety scissors around for smaller hands!

Brads: Some projects call for brass brads to hold pieces together. If you do not have those on hand, you can substitute with twist ties.

Art supplies: Children can use crayons, markers, or paint to color these projects. If children will be painting, be aware that acrylic paint will dry permanently, though when wet it is easily cleaned up with water. Make sure children clean painting tools thoroughly when they are finished painting.

Art smock: Make sure children wear smocks or old shirts to protect clothes while working with paints and other messy materials.

Flex Time

Another great thing about the crafts, coloring pages, and writing pages in this book is that they provide for versatility—which definitely comes in handy when working with children of differing skill levels. The crafts can be simplified or made more complex depending on need.

Coloring pages are simple enough for younger children, but older children may want to challenge themselves by adding patterns, textures, or even decorations. Likewise, the writing pages are great for older children to let their imaginations flow in creating original stories, while beginning writers may use them to copy a few words or dictate longer stories to an adult. If your group is of mixed ages, consider taking a teamwork approach that combines the imaginative approach of a younger child and the writing skills of an older child.

Great Clips

Clip-art pages are great for all kinds of applications. You can use a copy machine to increase the size of the seasonal images to make them suitable for wall or bulletin board decorations. Likewise, you can use the copier to make images smaller for use on worksheets, bulletins, notes to parents, or any other application you can dream up. Incorporate the clip-art images to create seasonal birthday cards or stationery, or use them to add a decorative element to any other project.

In the Mix

All of the projects presented in this book, from the simplest to the most elaborate, are just ideas to get you started. Feel free to alter the designs by choosing different materials or embellishing in any number of unique ways. Give your imagination free rein as you play around with materials and these base ideas. Encourage students to come up with their own unique variations on these themes, and keep them in mind for later uses. You can jump off in any direction, keeping these projects as fun and fresh as the first time you tried them. When it comes to creating fun summertime activities, the sky is the limit!

Summertime Bugs!

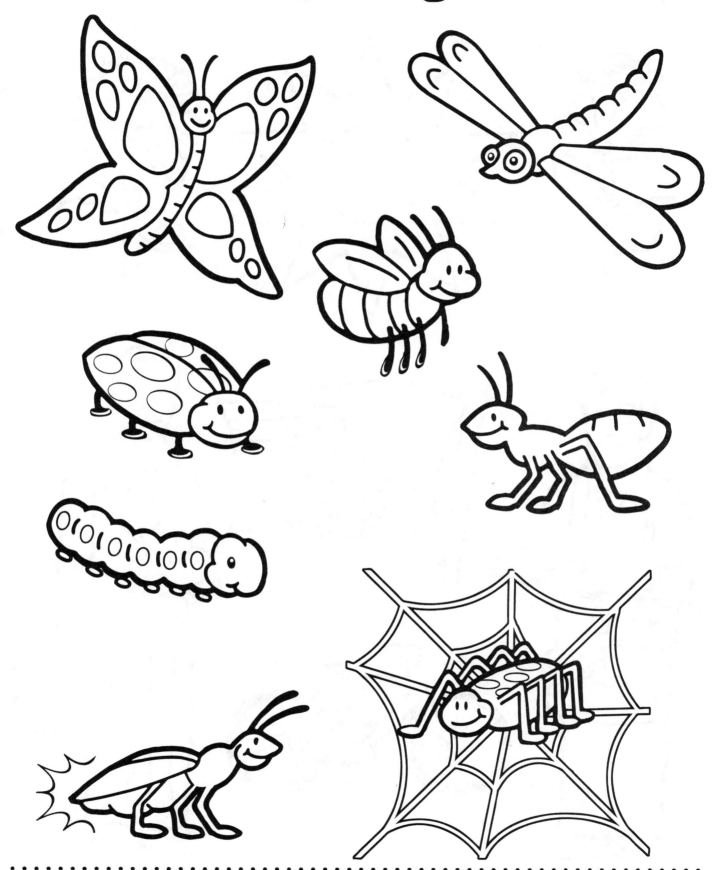

Special June Days

A Birthday Hat

Celebrate this month's birthdays with this fun hat. Color, cut out, and tape or glue the hat. Then use a piece of string to secure the hat around your chin.

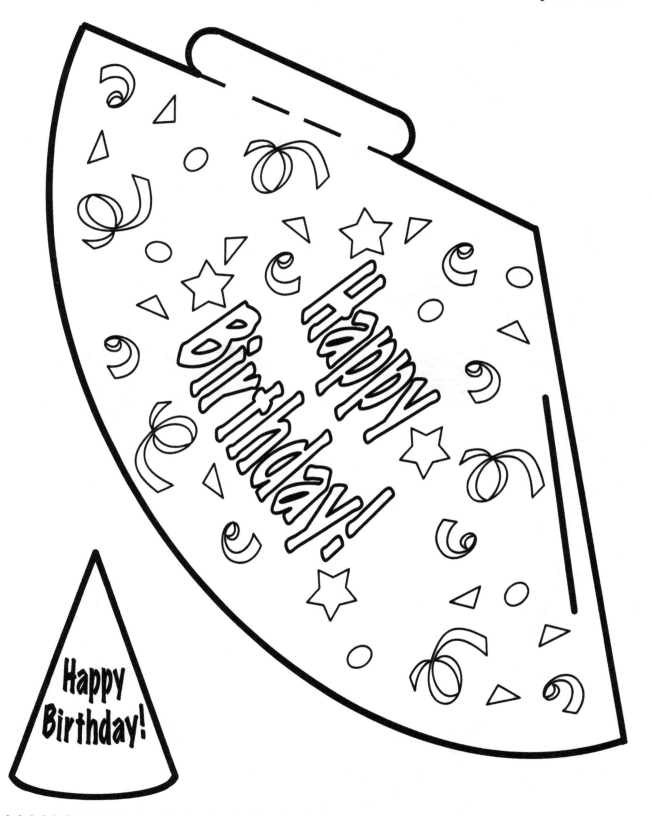

It's National Smile Month!

Something is missing from the face on this page. Can you color and cut out the face and the smiles and make sure the person is happy? Try putting each of the smiles on the face and pick your favorite!

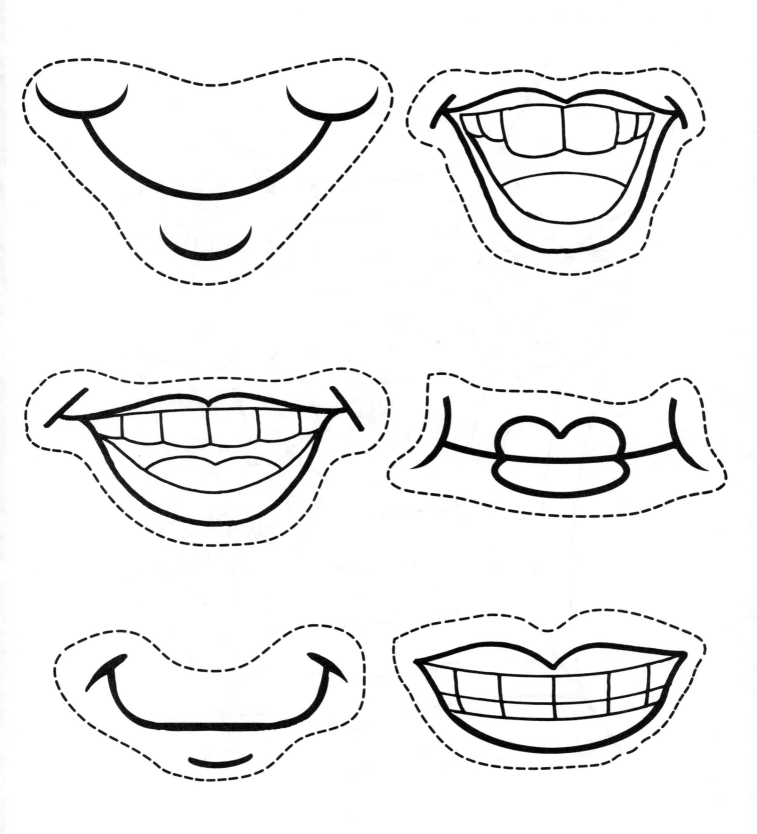

Web Site

Help the little bug cross the spiderwebs and avoid the spiders.

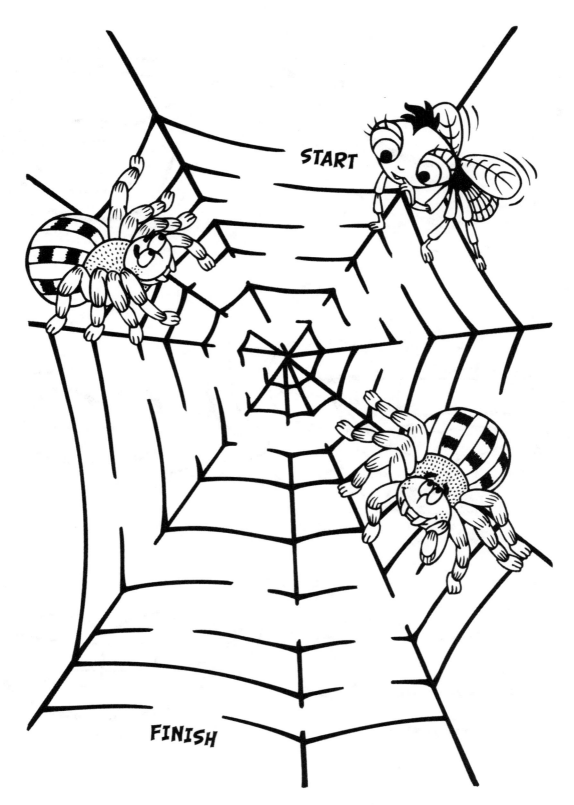

START

FINISH

Answer on page 96.

Donut Day!

Donuts are a neat breakfast treat. In June, you can celebrate Donut Day to honor this fun food. Make this donut delicious by coloring and decorating it. Paste on some glitter or confetti to add some scrumptious sprinkles!

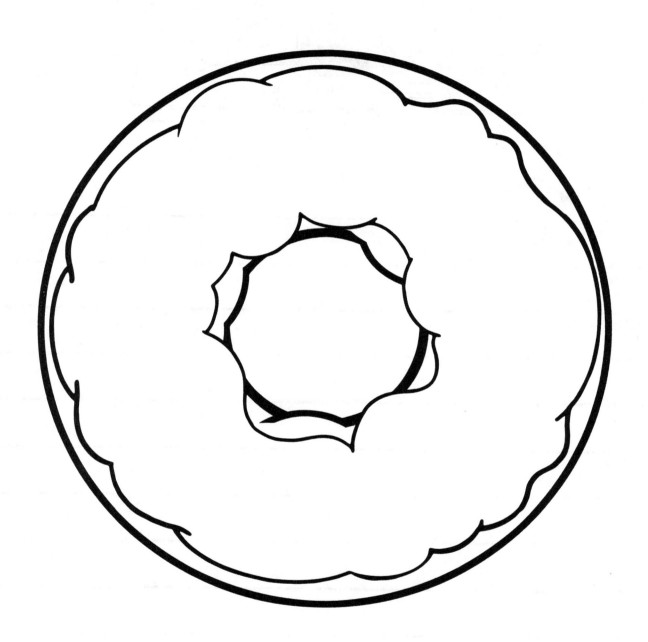

What I Learned This Year

Write about something fun or interesting you learned in school this year.

_____

_____

_____

_____

_____

_____

_____

_____

_____

_____

End of School Diploma

Congratulations!

has completed _____ grade!

Let's Play Soccer!

Soccer is a fun game to play outside. Now you can play inside, too! Color, cut out, and put together the soccer players and the goal. Make a soccer ball out of crumpled-up scrap paper and use the dolls to "kick" the ball into the goal. If you want, you can make two goals and challenge a friend to play against you!

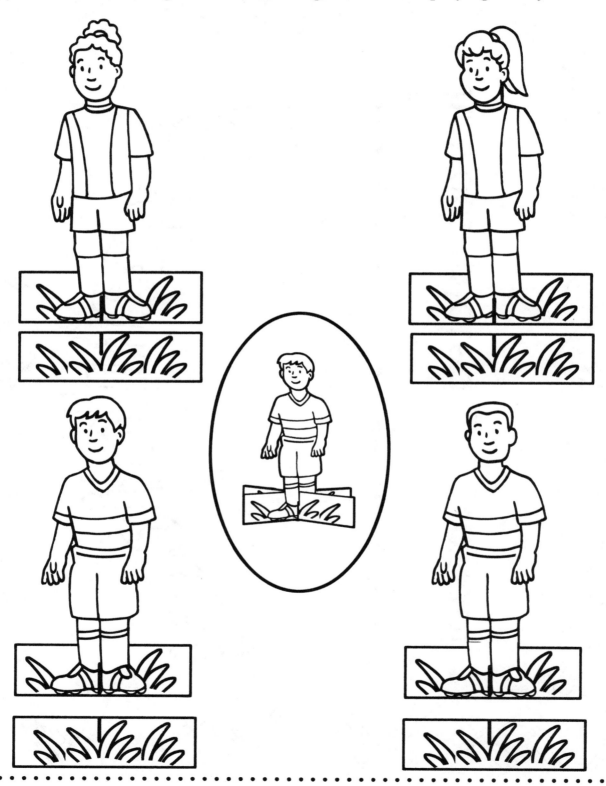

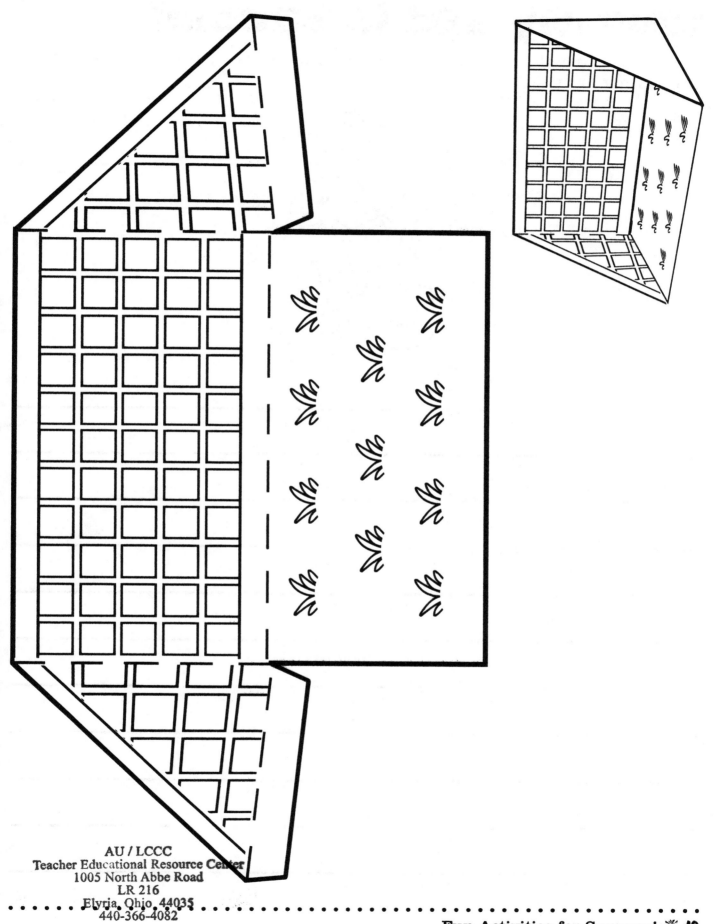

Why My Dad Is Special

Write to tell something special about your father. You can also write about a grandfather or uncle.

_____

_____

_____

_____

_____

_____

_____

_____

_____

A Father's Day Card

Here is a Father's Day card you can color, decorate, and give to your dad or someone special! You can write a message or draw a picture inside of the card.

A Father's Day Ribbon

This is a special prize to let your dad know how special he is to you! Decorate it with your dad's favorite colors. On the strands of the ribbon, write words that tell why your dad is special.

It's National Candy Month

June is National Candy Month! To celebrate, you can color and cut out these pieces of candy. Put a string through the end of each piece to make your own candy necklace.

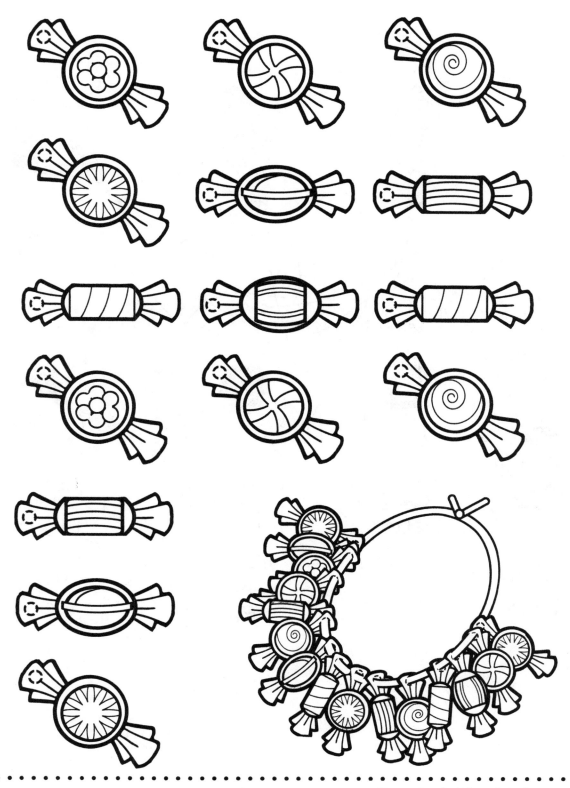

Whose Kite Am I?

What a windy day! These four friends were just in the park, flying their kites, when a huge gust of wind tangled the strings. Can you figure out which kite belongs to which person? (Be careful! The kite strings will cross each other.)

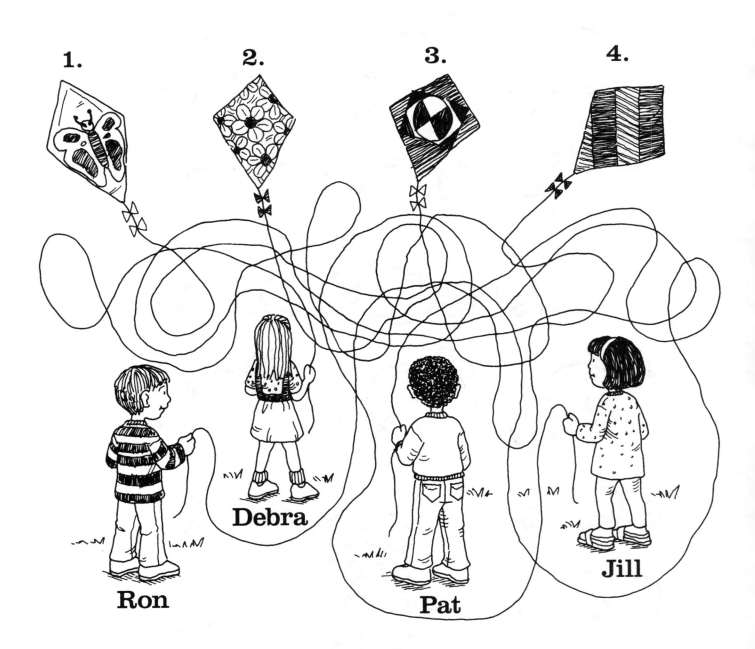

Answers on page 96.

It's Flag Day!

Every June 14 we honor the American flag with Flag Day. Color this flag so it's ready to fly for Flag Day!

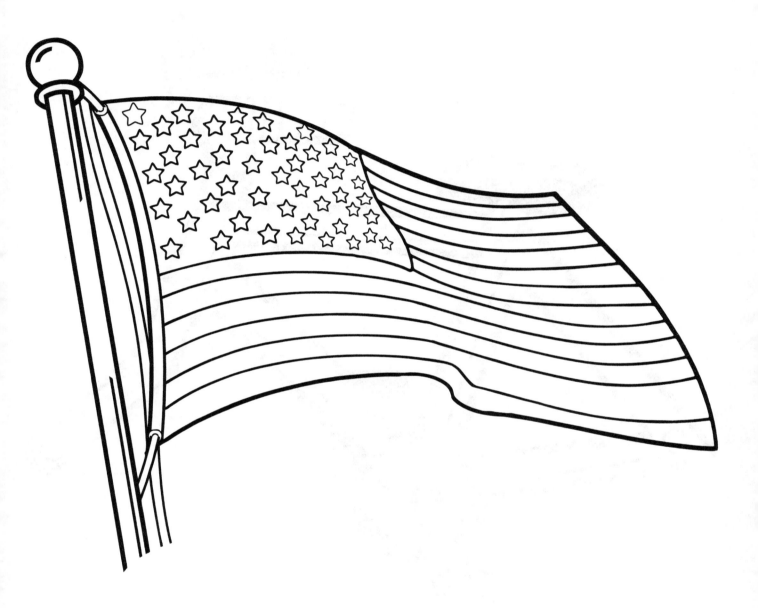

Build a Bicycle

Get ready to bike! Color and cut out the pieces of the bicycle. Then, attach the wheels to the frame of the bicycle. If you have them, use metal fasteners so the wheels of the bicycle can spin. You can also use tape or glue, if you like.

My Picnic Story

Write a story about a fun picnic you have enjoyed. You can also make up a fun picnic story!

_____

_____

_____

_____

_____

_____

_____

_____

_____

_____

A Big Barbecue

Something sure smells good! Color and cut out the grill and all of the food so you can cook up your favorite barbecue treats.

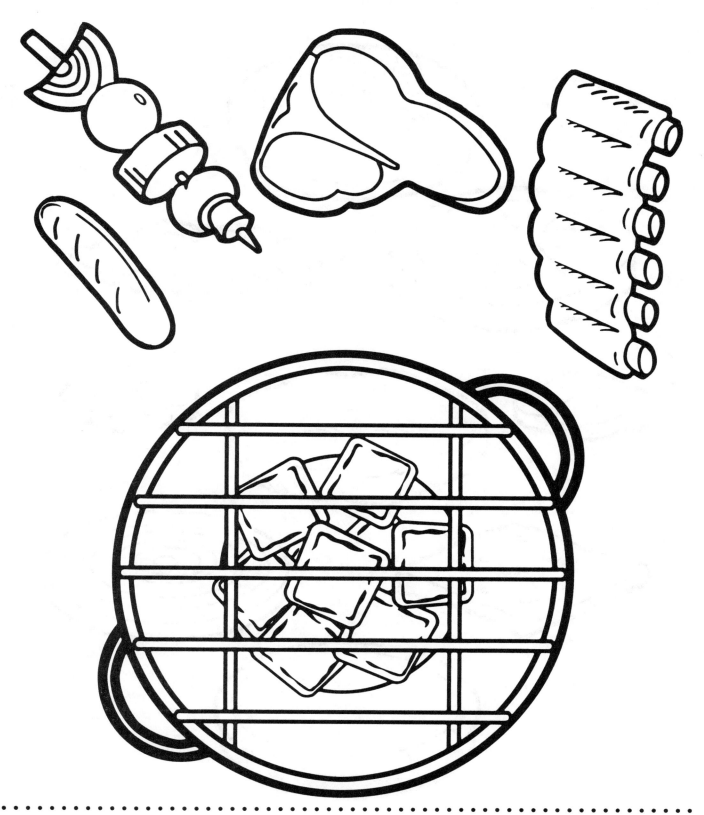

That's One Tasty Burger!

This hamburger looks delicious, but you have to put it together before you can eat it! Color and cut out the hamburger, bun, and toppings. Then, stack everything up to build your own tasty burger.

A Summer Storm

Summer has lots of sunny days, but sometimes it can be cloudy and rainy. Once in a while, the weather gets really wild and you get big storms with thunder and lightning! Color and cut out these clouds, lightning bolts, and rain gear. String them together to create your own rainy day display!

Get Ready to Fish!

This boy and girl are getting ready to go fishing. Help them prepare by coloring and decorating their clothes. After you finish coloring, cut out the boy and girl.

Let's Go Fishing!

It's time to get a line in the water and go fishing! Color the fish and the pond, then cut them out. Tape or glue paper clips to the backs of the fish and lay them in the pond. Then, tie a piece of string to the end of a pencil and attach the other end of the string to a small magnet to make your own fishing pole. Use the fishing dolls that you made before with your new fishing pole to catch the fish!

Splish Splash

Can you find the 17 differences between the top and the bottom pool scenes?

Answers on page 96.

Summer Vacation!

The 4th of July

A Birthday Certificate

Celebrate this month's birthdays with this fun certificate. Color and cut out the certificate, and then write your name on the line if you have a July birthday!

Happy Birthday!

_____

is ____ years old today!

It's National Hot Dog Month!

Did you know that July is National Hot Dog Month? You can join in the fun by decorating this hot dog stand! Write your name on the sign and draw yourself working. You can write the menu and draw hot dogs or other foods you like, too!

Mighty Monument

Below is one of the most popular monuments in the United States. See if you can finish the monument by connecting the dots 1 through 18.

Answer on page 96.

My 4th of July

How do you like to celebrate the 4th of July? Write about something you like to do for this holiday.

_____

_____

_____

_____

_____

_____

_____

_____

_____

_____

U.S. Postage Stamp Day

July 1 is U.S. Postage Stamp Day! Stamps have all kinds of pictures on them. What would you like to see on a stamp? In the outline you can draw a special stamp to honor somebody you think is a hero or just somebody you like a lot!

Watch the Fireworks!

Do you know what else happens on the 4th of July? Fireworks! In the sky below use colorful crayons or markers to make your own exciting fireworks display.

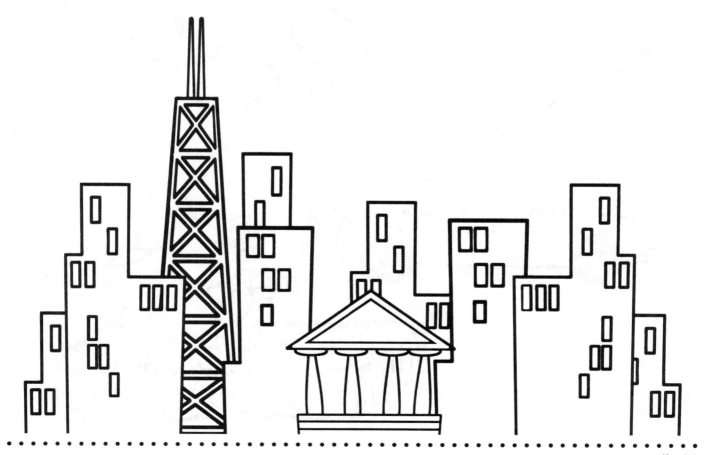

The 4th of July Parade!

Lots of people go see parades to celebrate the 4th of July. Color and cut out all of the pictures below. You can then arrange your own parade!

A Beach Puzzle!

Prepare to be puzzled! Color the picture below and cut it into the pieces of a jigsaw puzzle. Mix up the pieces and then put the picture back together again!

A Day at the Beach

This beach looks empty! Can you bring everyone back to the beach? Draw and color some people, animals, boats, toys, and whatever else you would like to see at the beach in the space below!

Fun in the Water and Sun!

Write about a fun trip you could take to a beach, pool, or water park.

_____

_____

_____

_____

_____

_____

_____

_____

_____

_____

It's National Ice Cream Month!

July is National Ice Cream Month! Nothing beats a cool treat on a hot summer day. Color and cut out the cone and ice cream scoops. Try to decorate the scoops so they look like your favorite ice cream flavors! Add sprinkles in your favorite colors.

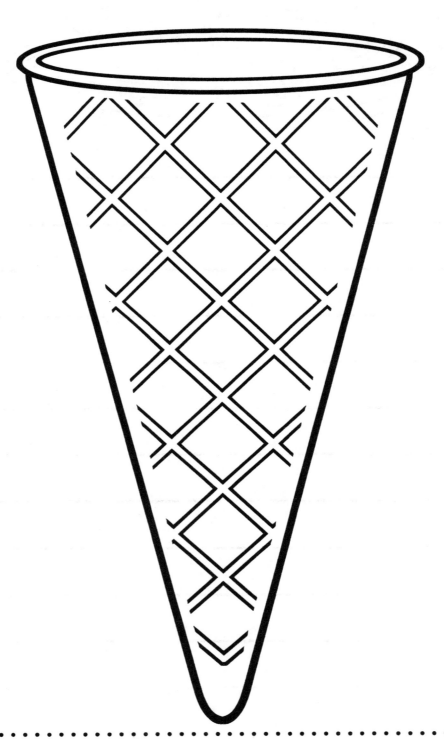

Wild Wally's Water Park

Jump on an inner tube, and slide through the maze to the tropical lagoon.

Answer on page 96.

A Trip to the Ballpark

Write about a baseball game that you have played or watched. You can also write about another sport that you enjoy!

_____

_____

_____

_____

_____

_____

_____

_____

_____

_____

_____

Summer Sports

Summer is a great time to go outside and play sports. Color and cut out the boy and girl and their clothes. Dress them so they're ready to play your favorite summer sport! Then try all of the other clothes!

Summer Flowers

One of the best things about summer is all of the beautiful flowers! Color and cut out the flowers and flowerpot. Add straws or pipe cleaners to the backs of the flowers to make stems. Then, use tape or glue to arrange all of your flowers in the flowerpot!

Cows and Cowboys!

Did you know that July 25 is Cow Appreciation Day and National Day of the Cowboy? Celebrate this fun day by coloring and cutting out the cows, cowboy, and fences. Hang everything up and make a neat mobile!

It's Picnic Time!

This family looks like it's ready to dig in and enjoy a picnic, but something is missing! Can you draw and color a tasty picnic lunch for them? You can draw all of your favorite picnic foods!

Starry Night

Summer nights are a great time to go outside and look up at the stars. Color and cut out all of the pictures below. Arrange and paste them all on a black piece of paper to make your own starry night scene. Then you can stargaze any time you like!

Pack for Your Trip!

Many people spend their summer vacation by going on a trip. You can't travel until you pack your bags! Color and decorate the stickers with words or pictures that tell about a place you have been to or somewhere you would like to go. Also color the suitcase and cut everything out. Tape or glue the stickers on your suitcase and get ready to hit the road!

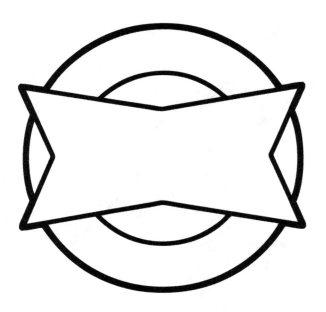

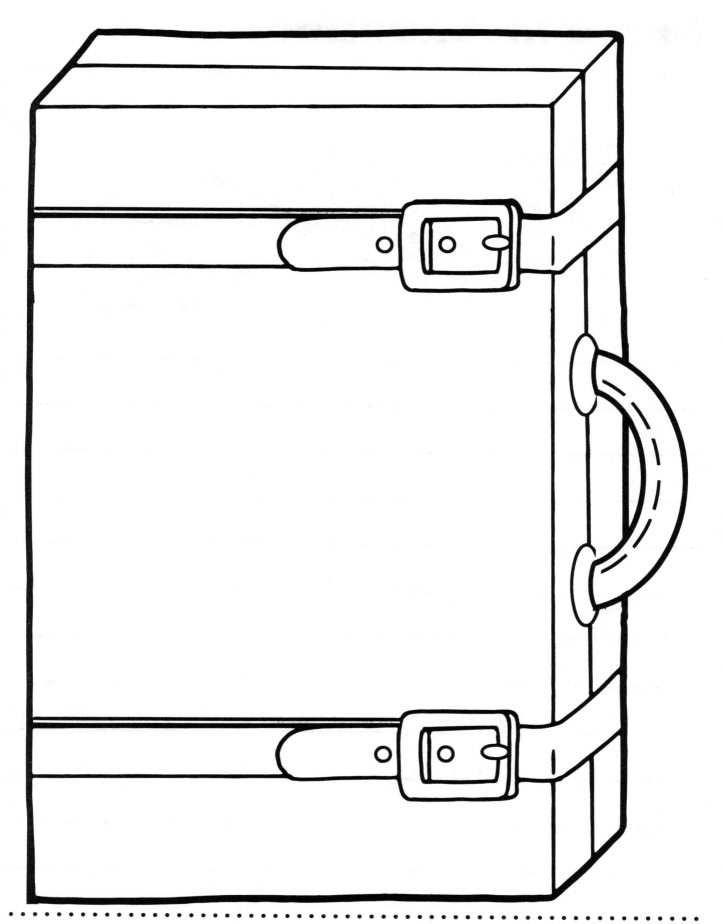

Going on Vacation!

Going on vacation is fun! Write about a trip you have taken or would like to take.

_____

_____

_____

_____

_____

_____

_____

_____

_____

_____

It's a Hot One Today

All 10 words in the word list are hidden in the sun-shape grid below. Look across, down, and diagonally to find these words about the weather. Circle each word in the grid as you find it, and then cross it off the word list. We circled *WET* to get you started.

CLOUDY   SLEET

DAMP   STORM

HAIL   THUNDER

HOT   ~~WET~~

LIGHTNING   WIND

```
                    S
   S                L                    U
      N          W E T             R
         H A E H I
         N A S T O R M
   T O L I G H T N I N G
         C L O U D Y R
         W I N D A
         N   A D D   M
   O             E         P
                 R
```

August

Summer Fun!

Let's Go Camping!

A Magical Birthday!

Celebrate this month's birthdays with this fun birthday wand. Color and cut out the wand for everyone with an August birthday!

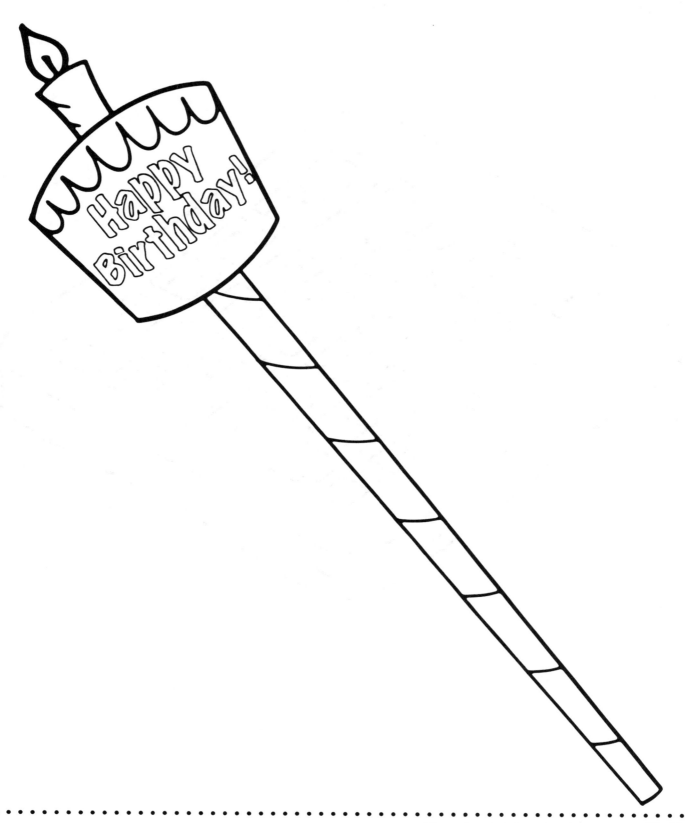

Waffle Week!

Did you know that the first week of August is Waffle Week? Color and cut out the waffle and toppings, and then put them all together. If you don't see your favorite topping, you can draw it yourself!

A Sunny Day Seek

Can you find these 13 items hidden in the picture?

Answers on page 96.

How I Beat the Heat!

Write about something you do to stay cool in the summertime.

_____

_____

_____

_____

_____

_____

_____

_____

_____

Build a Lighthouse

August 7 is Lighthouse Day! Celebrate this fun day by making your own lighthouse. Color and cut out the pieces on the next page, and then attach the buildings to this island with tape or glue.

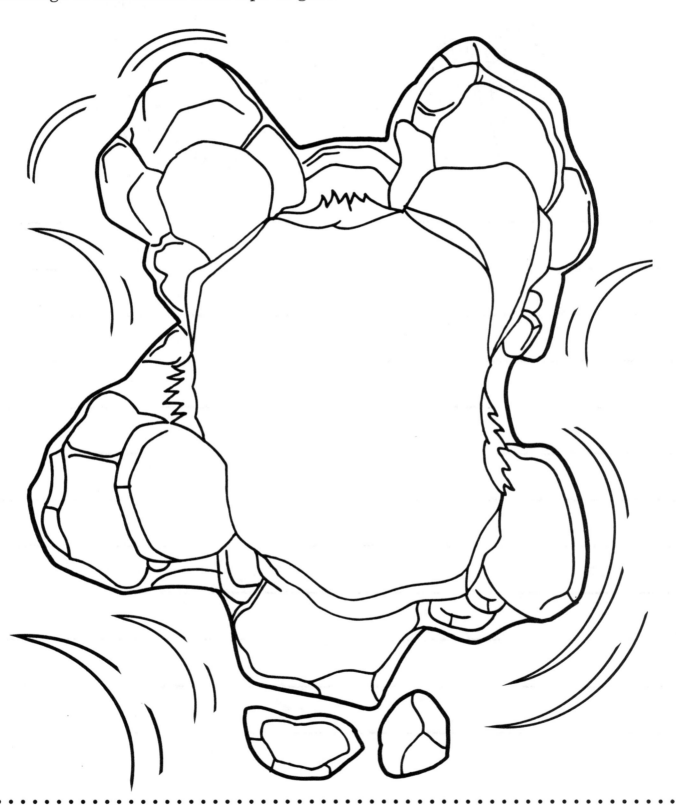

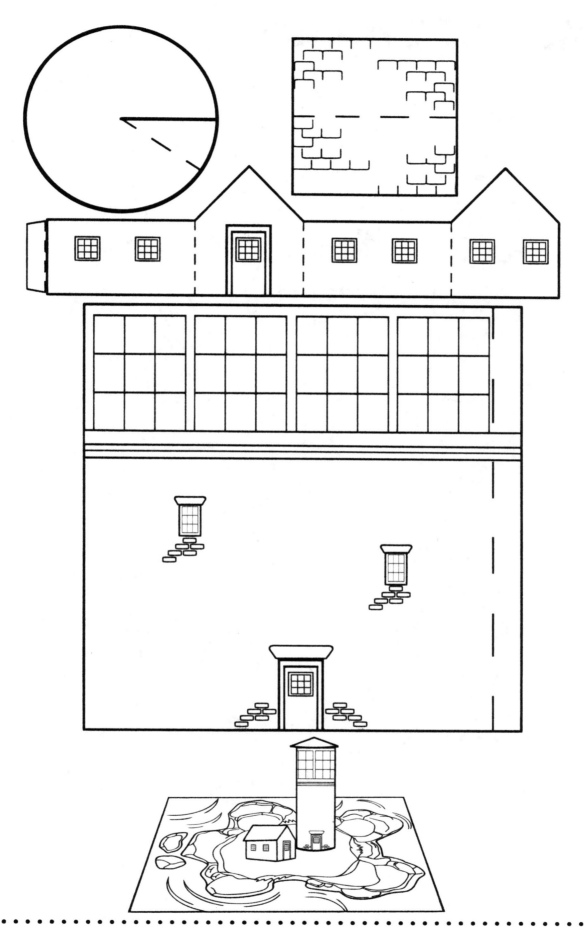

Pairs of Twins!

Did you know that August 7 is also Twins Day? Color the children and help each set of twins find one another by drawing a line connecting them. You can also cut them out and match them up, if you like!

Time to Play!

The playground is a fun place to go in the summer! Color the playground and draw yourself and your friends playing on your favorite playground equipment!

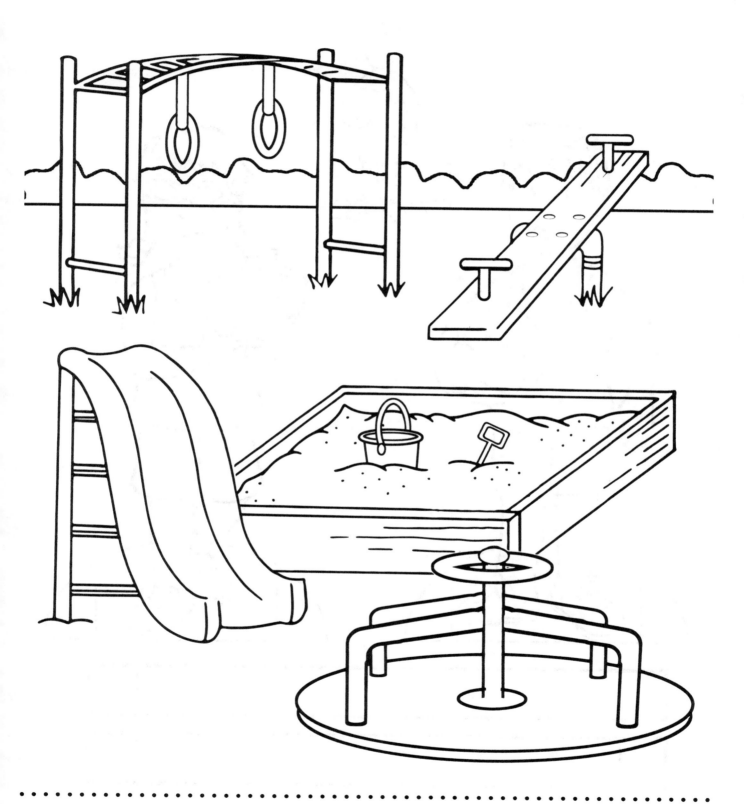

Volleyball Fun!

Volleyball is a great game to play at the beach or in your own backyard! Color and cut out the volleyball players and their net. Set up the net and use a small ball of scrap paper to play volleyball whenever you want!

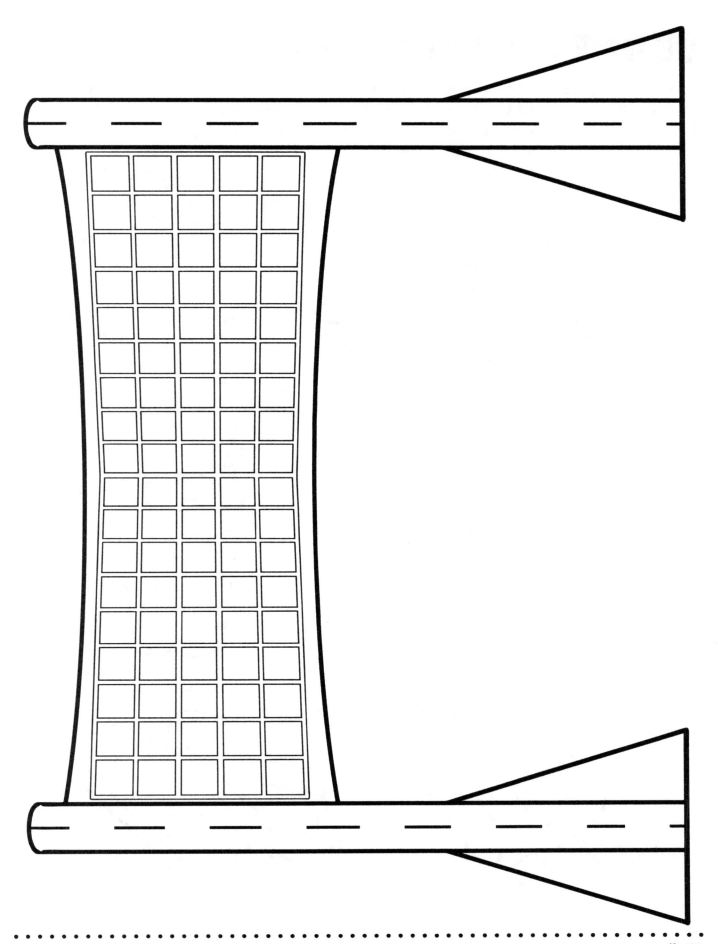

What a Sunny Day!

There's nothing better than a nice, sunny day! Now you can enjoy the best things about a sunny day all the time! Color and cut out all of the sunny day pictures below. String them all together to make your own sunny day display!

What I Like to Do Outside

Write about your favorite thing to do outside during the summer.

_____

_____

_____

_____

_____

_____

_____

_____

_____

_____

It's Cupcake Day!

August 18 is Cupcake Day! To celebrate, cut out and decorate the cupcake. You can color it and attach some fun sprinkles or glitter with glue!

Sunny Day

Pull out your crayons or markers. Color the circles yellow, the squares blue, the triangles red, and the rectangles green. Fill in the rest of the scene with whatever colors you want.

Write a Postcard!

It's fun to send and receive postcards! Decorate the postcard and write a note to a friend about somewhere you went this summer or something fun you did. Once you finish both sides of the postcard you can tape or glue them together with a piece of card stock in the middle. Ask a grown-up for help if you'd like to mail it!

Gather Around the Campfire

Summer is a great time to go camping. When people go camping, they build campfires to cook food and stay warm at night. Color and decorate the campfire and the campfire items. Then you can cut out the campfire items and add them to the scene around the fire!

In My Tent!

You can't go camping without a tent! Inside the tent, draw yourself and a friend or relative you would like to come with you on a camping trip.

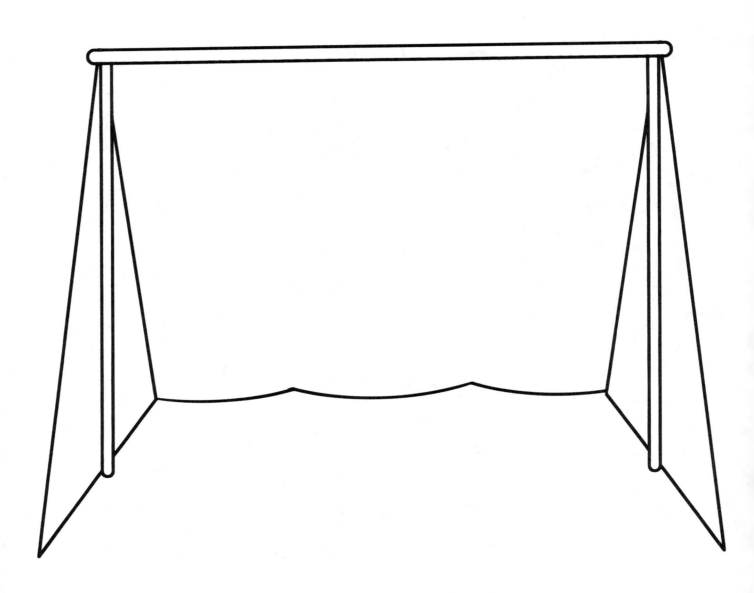

Fan the Heat Away

Fans help people stay cool during the summer. Decorate the fan with a fun drawing or design. Attach a wooden stick, pencil, or plastic straw to use as a handle.

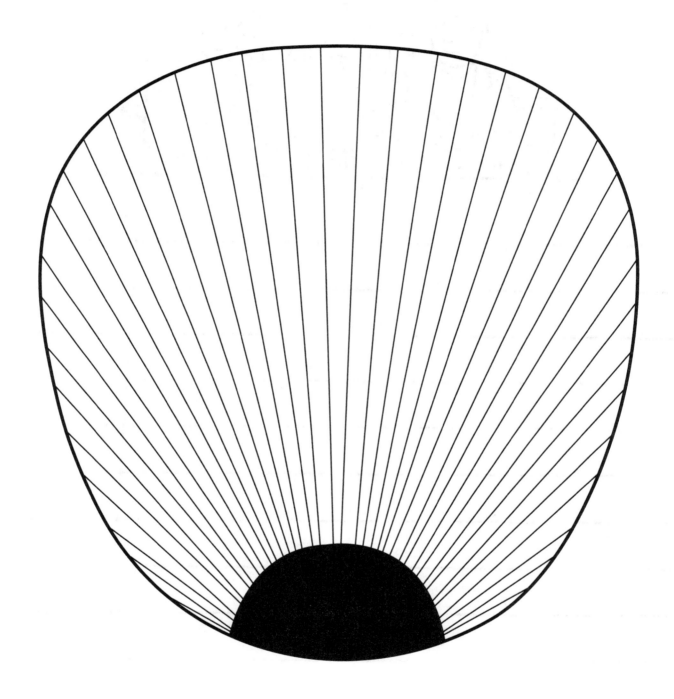

My Amazing Invention!

Write about something you could invent to make life better for everyone!

_____

_____

_____

_____

_____

_____

_____

_____

_____

_____

My Best Friend!

Did you know that part of August is Friendship Week? In the frame, draw a picture of what you and your best friend like to do when you are together!

A Cool Pair of Shades!

Keep the summer sun out of your eyes with your own pair of sunglasses! Color and cut out the parts of the sunglasses and glue or tape them together. If you have some colored cellophane, use it to make lenses for your shades!

Fruit Salad

All 8 fruits in the word list are hidden in the berry-shape grid below. Look across, down, and diagonally. Circle each word in the grid as you find it, and cross it off the word list. We circled *BANANA* to get you started.

~~BANANA~~
BERRY
GRAPE
MELON

ORANGE
PEACH
PEAR
PLUM

```
    H   I
        O
        R
    P   E   A   C   H
G  (B   A   N   A   N   A)
G   E   P   G   N   P   E
C   R   M   E   L   O   N
T   R   A   U   A   A   R
    Y   M   P   I   R
    N   E   E
```

Answers on page 96.

A Trip to the Zoo!

Summer is a great time to visit the zoo and see lots of animals! What is your favorite animal to see at the zoo? Draw the animals you like best and color their zoo home.

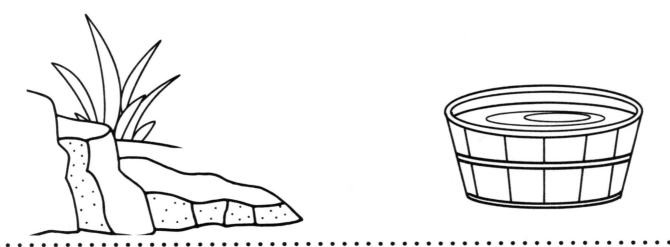

Animals and Their Babies

Can you help these animal babies find their parents? Color all of the animals and draw a line between each baby animal and its parent. You can also cut out the animals and match them up, if you like.

Answers

Web Site *(page 14)*

Mighty Monument
(page 42)

It's a Hot One Today *(page 65)*

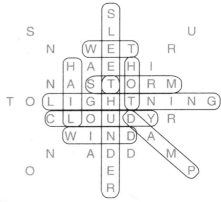

Whose Kite Am I?
(page 24)
Ron, 2; Debra, 3; Pat, 1;
Jill, 4

Splish Splash
(page 36)

Wild Wally's Water Park *(page 52)*

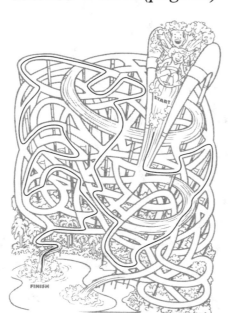

A Sunny Day Seek
(page 72)

Fruit Salad *(page 93)*

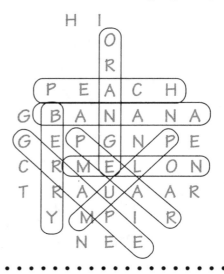

AU / LCCC
Teacher Educational Resource Center
1005 North Abbe Road
LR 216
Elyria, Ohio 44035
440-366-4082